They Shall Mount up with Wings

They Shall Mount up with Wings

Lance Lambert

LANCE LAMBERT MINISTRIES

Richmond, Virginia, USA

Previously published by:
Two-fish Publications
Corona, California

ISBN:978-1-68389-088-1
www.lancelambert.org

Contents

Introduction

"They shall mount up with wings..."
This title, taken from the 40th chapter of Isaiah, was written to help those who were in the faithful remnant in Israel during a time when the country was beginning to backslide. The prophet speaks of people fainting, having no strength, and being unable to face the downward spiral. It is a marvelous word to every one of us in these tumultuous times: He giveth power to the faint and increaseth strength to those who have no might (40:29). So there is much hope in whatever conditions we might find ourselves and whatever we are now moving into. As Isaiah spoke, in the light of the coming of the Messiah, to encourage God's people to remain faithful, and to know the Lord, so it is also a comfort to us who are expectantly waiting for our Lord's return.*[1]

---

1 These three messages were given in June of 2011

1.
The Everlasting Word of God

Isaiah 40:1–31

Comfort ye, comfort ye my people, saith your God. Speak ye comfortably to Jerusalem; and cry unto her, that her warfare is accomplished, that her iniquity is pardoned, that she hath received of the Lord's hand double for all her sins. The voice of one that crieth, Prepare ye in the wilderness the way of the Lord; make level in the desert a highway for our God. Every valley shall be exalted, and every mountain and hill shall be made low; and the uneven shall be made level, and the rough places a plain: and the glory of the Lord shall be revealed, and all flesh shall see it together; for the mouth of the Lord hath spoken it.

The voice of one saying, Cry. And one said, What shall I cry? All flesh is grass, and all the goodliness thereof is as the flower of the field. The grass withereth, the flower fadeth, because the breath of the Lord bloweth upon it; surely the people is grass. The grass withereth, the flower fadeth; but the word of our God shall stand forever.

O thou that tellest good tidings to Zion, get thee up on a high mountain; O thou that tellest good tidings to Jerusalem, lift up thy voice with strength; lift it up, be not afraid; say unto the cities of Judah, Behold, your God! Behold, the Lord God will come as a mighty one, and his arm will rule for him: Behold, his reward is with him, and his recompense before him. He will feed his flock like a shepherd, he will gather the lambs in his arm, and carry them in his bosom, and will gently lead those that have their young.

Who hath measured the waters in the hollow of his hand, and meted out heaven with the span, and comprehended the dust of the earth in a measure, and weighted the mountains in scales, and the hills in a balance? Who hath directed the Spirit of the Lord, or being his counsellor hath taught him? With whom took he counsel, and who instructed him, and taught him in the path of justice, and taught him knowledge, and showed to him the way of understanding? Behold, the nations are as a drop of a bucket, and are accounted as the small dust of the balance: behold, he taketh up the isles as a very little thing. And Lebanon is not sufficient to burn, nor the beasts thereof sufficient for a burnt-offering. All the nations are as nothing before him; they are accounted by him as less than nothing, and vanity.

To whom then will ye liken God? or what likeness will ye compare unto him? The image, a workman hath cast it and the goldsmith overlayeth it with gold, and casteth for it silver chains. He that is too impoverished for such an oblation chooseth a tree that will not rot; he seeketh unto him a skillful workman to set up a graven image that shall not be moved. Have ye not known? Have ye not heard? hath it not been told you from the beginning? have ye not understood from the foundations of the earth? It is he that sitteth above the circle of the earth, and the inhabitants thereof are as grasshoppers; that stretcheth out the heavens as a curtain, and spreadeth them out as a tent to dwell in; that bringeth princes to nothing; that maketh the judges of the earth as vanity. Yea, they have not been planted; yea, they have not been sown; yea, their stock hath not taken root in the earth:

moreover he bloweth upon them, and they wither, and the whirlwind taketh them away as stubble. To whom then will ye liken me, that I should be equal to him? saith the Holy One. Lift up your eyes on high, and see who hath created these, that bringeth out their host by number; he calleth them all by name; by the greatness of his might, and for that he is strong in power, not one is lacking. Why sayest thou, O Jacob, and speakest, O Israel, My way is hid from the Lord, and the justice due to me is passed away from my God? Hast thou not known? hast thou not heard? The everlasting God, Jehovah, the Creator of the ends of the earth, fainteth not, neither is weary; there is no searching of his understanding. He giveth power to the faint; and to him that hath no might he increaseth strength. *Even the youths shall faint and be weary, and the young men shall utterly fall: but they that wait for the Lord shall renew their strength; they shall mount up with wings as eagles; they shall run, and not be weary; they shall walk, and not faint.*

Just a word of prayer:

Beloved Lord, we are so thankful that we are gathered in Your presence, and when we are in Your presence anything can happen. There is nothing too hard for You, nothing too difficult, nothing impossible. There is no advance You cannot make and no purpose that You cannot achieve and fulfill. We want to thank You and worship You, Lord, and ask that You will make this a time when we meet with Yourself. Manifest Your presence among us. We thank You for the anointing, grace and power that You have won for us at Calvary, and into that grace and power we stand by faith for the speaking of Your word and for the hearing of Your word. Let this be an anointed time, a time when You are here in all Your fullness with a double portion of that anointing upon us all. And we shall be careful to give You all the praise and all the worship of our hearts for answering this prayer which we ask in the name of our Messiah, the Lord Jesus. Amen.

This passage in Isaiah has been on my heart in the last day or two and I have become aware that the Lord, in some way, wants to communicate it and write it upon our hearts.

We are aware that we are moving very swiftly and strongly into a period of shaking such as we have never known before—a period of turmoil, conflict and darkness.

If that is the case, are we going to be strong enough, not merely to be survivors, but to be overcomers? There is a whole number of opinions floating around concerning what lies ahead of us. Will things get better? Will we return to the boom years in the economy? Will there be stability in finance once again? Will the climate settle down from a kind of series of hiccups through which it has passed in the last year or two? I think it is clear, at least to me, that we are moving into a period that the Scriptures call "the judgment of the nations." That does not mean men and women will not be saved, for Joel tells us in his prophecy: "Whosoever shall call upon the name of the Lord shall be saved" (see Joel 2:32). And he speaks that in the context of pillars of smoke and fire, and things happening in the sun, the moon and the stars. In the New Testament the Lord Jesus spoke about the seas and the billows of the seas and men's hearts failing for fear. We are not quite there yet, but when we watched that terrible earthquake in Fukushima, and the tsunami that followed, I think there was a kind of shudder that went through human society. Then we saw the floods in Australia which covered an area as large as France and Germany put together. I believe what lies at the root of all this is an attitude—especially in the Western Nations—towards the Word of God and the Law of God.

The Two Witnesses

Israel

I would also add to that the two witnesses; one is physical and the other is spiritual. The physical witness is the Jewish people. Israel was recreated as a nation and a state after the worst period ever in her thousands of years of history—the Holocaust. Out of the ashes of the Holocaust Israel was born. I cannot believe that there are Christian teachers and preachers who say that was a political accident and nothing whatsoever to do with the hand of God. I say it is a sign of the absolute trustworthiness of God's prophetic word, every single thing right down to the detail.

Now it is not my burden at this time to talk about Israel, but I do have to say that everything from the recreation of the Sanhedrin exactly as it was, with its layout, its way of acting, and so on, is amazing. The recreation of the fertility of Israel from desert to forest, to groves of olive trees, of citrus fruits, fields everywhere, the restoration of the ecology, the restoration of the former and latter rains are truly extraordinary. It is a testimony to the nations.

Of course, Israel continues in unbelief. She has rejected the Messiah, and even now at present is in that stance. However, there are more Jews (we call them Messianic Jews) who have been born and saved by the grace of God today than at any time since the first half-century of the church. But the fact still remains that this is a physical nation with an army, an air force, a navy, a parliament and all the various things that are normally to do with a state. But we once again see anti-Semitism growing in the most incredible manner—in Western Europe particularly. The nations are alienated from Israel. They began by praising her and being sympathetic to her because of the Holocaust and the fact that she was surrounded by 200 million Muslims with five armies, three of them trained and armed by the British. It was truly a David and Goliath situation. On the whole the nations tended to be sympathetic; but that has all disappeared now. Mahmoud Abbas says that 180 nations have recognized the Palestinians as a sovereign state—in other words, it is the division of the Promised Land.

Listen! You cannot contradict a covenant that God made with Abraham. God is not past and future; He is present, if you understand what I mean. He said, *My name is I AM. I AM that I AM.* In other words, there is no past or future; it is all present. It was as if yesterday or a week ago the Lord made this covenant with Abraham and confirmed it with Isaac and Jacob. He said that whilst there is a generation alive of this physical seed of Abraham, this covenant is operative and functional (see Genesis 17:7).

There is no room for the leaders of the nations to come and say: "You made a mistake; this is not just. It does not give ground for human rights. We must change it. We will divide the Promised Land into two states." This is *not* an option. If any nation decides to cancel God's covenant and divide the Promised Land—whether it is the President of the United States, the American administration, Britain, Russia, the United Nations, or the Quartet—they have set themselves immediately on a collision course with the Almighty. And that is exactly what is happening.

We hear everywhere that it is human error and mismanagement that has caused the climate problem. I am not sure about that. They tell us about this warming, and suddenly, we find that we are having the coldest weather we have had for decades in China, in northern Europe, in Western Europe, and here in the States as well. I believe it is God. The Almighty Himself is turning the whole climate conditions of the world upside down, and far worse is to come. If I read my Bible correctly, there will soon be signs in the sun, and following that, of course, there will be changes in the moon and stars which will affect the seasons and the tides of the sea. Thus we begin to see a whole picture developing.

You might say, "How are we going to get through this?" That is a good question! It is one thing to read it in the Bible, it is another thing to live in it and see it actually happening. Are we going to be overcomers?

The True Church

The other witness is the true church. Many of the constitutions of the nations, particularly in the West, were formed by enormous awakenings. Hundreds of thousands got saved and were truly born of God. It changed the whole face of Europe, whether it was Germany or France with the Huguenots, Britain with all the incredible things that happened there, Scandinavia, Norway, Sweden, Denmark or the Netherlands. Out of those awakenings came a Constitution that is now being dismantled in every European country in Britain and the United States. It is no longer *Christmas* and *Christmas Greetings*; it is *Season's Greetings*. It has become an "it". It is called a *Winter Festival* and no longer a celebration of the birth of the Lord Jesus. Good Friday is nothing. We are not even allowed symbols of Christianity, although everything else is acceptable.

I believe you cannot do that without judgment. Whether we talk about gay rights, gay marriage, abortion, or any of these other things, they are a direct challenge to the Word of God and the Law of God. Now, is the God we worship, the Almighty, literally going to be someone who is just sort of deaf, dumb, and does nothing? Of course not! It seems to me that we are in for a very troubled period, and it will mean something for us all. As we observe this condition developing we might well ask: Where is God? Has He retired? Where is He? Furthermore, for faithful believers this current situation means stress and pressure in the atmosphere.

When Isaiah ministered this incredible prophecy, it was to a nation that by and large was departing from God. Much of it was lip service because they were spiritually blind. This amazing ministry of his was that even though all these things were taking place, this was his word: God's purpose to bring a Messiah to the world is going to be fulfilled. And even if there is only a faithful remnant in the country waiting for the Messiah and feeling the stress and the pressure during that time—Zacharias and Elizabeth, Simeon and Anna, the shepherds, Mary and Joseph, and maybe others—the fact of the matter is that God is going to fulfill His purpose on time exactly as He said.

Now we can take tremendous courage and strength from this because we are living in exactly the same kind of condition. We have a lukewarm church (that is putting it mildly), a church with wall-to-wall carpeting, ministers of education for the youth and the older ones, ministers of everything. We have great choirs, wonderful organs, orchestras, and entertainment galore. But there is not a single voice that speaks about judgment, as if it is no longer in the gospel. The idea we get sometimes is that to be a Christian one is carried on a flowery bed of ease into glory. We hear no talk about "through many tribulations we enter the kingdom of God" (see Acts 14:22b). There is no talk about the fellowship of His sufferings (see Philippians 3:10b), there is no talk about suffering for His name's sake. It is not even mentioned. We are living in such conditions.

Thank God, in the United States there is a faithful remnant all over this continent and Canada as well. And we can only praise the Lord for that kind of faithfulness. But it is only natural for believers to really wonder: "How am I going to face this? How am I going to come through this?" We older ones will soon go to be with the Lord, but the younger ones may face the full blast of what the Word of God calls the coming of the Antichrist and the preparation for his coming.

The Word of God Stands Forever

The first thing I want to say concerning this chapter is that the Word of God and the gospel of God is absolute; it is set in stone and you cannot change it. It is not only the everlasting Word of God, it is the everlasting gospel. "The grass withereth, the flower fadeth but the word of our God shall stand forever" (Isaiah 40:8). And then we find this: "O thou that tellest good tidings (in other words, it is the good news, the gospel) to Zion, get thee up on a high mountain; O thou that tellest good tidings to Jerusalem, lift up thy voice with strength; lift it up, be not afraid; say unto the cities of Judah, Behold your God!"

This is the first coming of the Lord Jesus. We could say: "Say to the cities of America, to the cities of Europe, to the cities of the world: 'Behold your God!'"

Everything is working on time; it is exactly as the Lord said. We have here the absolute trustworthiness of the Word of God. It does not matter what conditions we are going to face or find ourselves in or the circumstances that will surround us, the fact of the matter is that the Word of God—the statements, the declarations, and the promises of His Word—are trustworthy. "How many soever be the promises of God, in Christ is the yes: and through Him the Amen, to the glory of God" (see II Corinthians 1:20).

This means that this Book will be the same; it will not change in the way everything else is changing. This Word of God that we have from Genesis to Revelation—which they are trying to reinvent, recast, reform, bring up to date, make more contemporary, make more acceptable to modern society— is *the* Word of God, and it lives and abides forever. There is something thrilling about that and also about the gospel.

The Church that Makes the Lord Sick

It is so exciting to hear of many thousands coming to the Lord in Africa, in Southeast Asia, in China, in all the areas of the world that we once called the mission field. But in the home countries there is a Laodicean church and the Lord spoke of it saying: "You make me sick" (see Revelation 3:16b). It has been glossed up and put so beautifully: "I will spew you out of my mouth." It sounds so beautiful but in actual fact the Greek simply says: *You make me vomit. I am nauseated over you.*

I am sure that none of us want to be in that kind of condition. We do not want the Lord to be outside of an organization whether it is traditional, institutional, denominational, or evangelical. We do not want to be in an organization where the Lord Jesus Himself is outside knocking at the door and saying: "If any man hear my voice and open the door I will come in and sup with him and he with me." It is amazing to me that our Lord could be outside of the whole thing. The church in Laodicea had communion, they had the Lord's Table, all in the name of Jesus; they preached in His name and they preached about Him. This was not a church that had long ago departed from the Lord but it was one made up of born again believers in one of the wealthiest cities in the Roman Empire. This church was quite remarkable because the apostle Paul speaks very well of it in writing to the Colossians. He says: "Read the letter I have written to Laodicea and make sure they read the one that you have received from me" (see Colossians 4:16). It seems clear that the apostle at that point thought they were having problems; nevertheless, he thought well of both of these assemblies. They had prayer meetings, Bible studies, and evangelistic outreaches, but Jesus was outside and His estimate of them is unbelievable. He said: "You say, I am rich, I have got great wealth and riches, and I have need of nothing. But I say you are poor, you are wretched, miserable, blind and naked" (see Revelation 3:17). How in the world can a church have such an estimate of itself and the Lord's genuine estimate of their condition be entirely different? Would you have ever thought that the Lord would say concerning born again believers that they are wretched, miserable, poor, blind and naked?

When we come to the so-called homeland of missions—and I am not just speaking of the United States, but Europe,

Scandinavia, and the United Kingdom—there is really a small remnant of the faithful.

The Word Brings New Birth

This Word of God which we should treasure has brought new birth to us, for the apostle Peter says in his first letter:

> *Having been born again, not of corruptible seed, but of incorruptible, through the Word of God, which liveth and abideth. For all flesh is as grass, and all the glory thereof as the flower of grass. The grass withereth, and the flower falleth: but the word of the Lord abideth forever (1:23–24).*

What an amazing thing that every one of us who are born of God have been born through the Word of God.

The second thing is in Hebrews 4:12: "The Word of God is living, and active, and sharper than any two-edged sword … cutting in between soul and spirit." This is an amazing thing. Shakespeare is incredible for his works. The old English of King James is Shakespearean English. He was an incredible genius, but have you ever heard of someone being born again through Shakespeare? Or his or her life being illumined by some word from Shakespeare? Have you ever heard of an alcoholic being delivered through Shakespeare? Or a drug addict saved from his addiction? Or a divorced couple brought back together? Even the "Taming of the Shrew" does not do it. There is this marvelous thing we call absolute genius; but when the Spirit of God takes the Word of God and it enters into us we are saved and born of God. Something happens to us and in us.

One of the biggest troubles in the States is the thousands of people who think they are born of God, yet they are not. That is why the apostle said: Make your calling and election sure (II Peter 1:10). We need to be certain that we are truly born of God. What are the signs of being born of God through the Word of God? Our eyes are opened, and we begin to understand and see. Then we start to breathe and hunger and thirst. After that we start to crawl. This is all part of being a child of God. If none of that is evident, the person is not saved. They may be a church member; they may be baptized one way or another, but they are not saved.

There are certain evidences of a new birth. As we take notice of ourselves—older or younger—everything we have has come out of a few inches of flesh that was born years ago. Therefore, we see, we hear, we speak, we understand, and we walk. Spiritually, it is the same. When a person is born of God, they begin to hunger for the Lord; they hunger for fellowship with the Lord and with others. They are thirsty. They begin to breathe, and they begin to hear.

The Lord Jesus said: "My sheep hear my voice" (see John 10:3). I sometimes think that in many of our prayer meetings it is all a one-way conversation. We pour out our problems to the Lord, and if the Lord were to answer, we would drop dead!

There was a lady who used to be the plague of Halford House. She lived about eighty miles away and would phone regularly every few months. She tried always to speak to me. Now all the folks in Halford House, as soon as they heard her, tried to save me from her because they knew that I would never be able to say a word because the moment she got on the phone she poured out all her problems and never gave a chance for anyone say anything. But every now and again I would work late at night and there was nobody else in the place except me. The phone would ring, and when I took it up, it was her. She would explode and say, "Oh, praise the Lord, I have got you at last! The Lord has given you such a spirit of counsel and wisdom, and I have such problems." Then she would start pouring them out to me, but I could not get a word in even if I shouted. I learned after a while that the only thing to do was to take the phone, listen, and then put it quietly down and get on with my work. I would take it up a few minutes later and say "yes, yes," and put it down, and then a bit later take it up again. It was always about twenty or twenty-five minutes and she would then say, "Thank you, you have counseled me exactly as I thought you would! I am so glad for that counsel. God has graced you with wisdom." Then she would ring off; I never got a chance to say a single thing.

Our prayer meetings are much like this. We pour out everything to the Lord, but if the Lord tried to say anything back to us we would drop dead.

Equipped by the Word of God

Nevertheless, this Word of God is so amazing, and in II Timothy we find these words of Paul:

Every scripture inspired of God is also profitable for teaching, for reproof, for correction, for instruction which is in righteousness: that the man of God may be complete, furnished completely unto every good work (3:16–17).

Now that is a bit more than just a dead word that has been put on a shelf and taken down once in a while, dusted off and read; or maybe something one hears preached about in church. This is something tremendous! We are equipped by the Word of God; it actually does something to us when it gets into us. The word becomes flesh. "May the word of Christ dwell in you richly in all wisdom" (Colossians 3:16a). This Word of God corrects us, realigns us, causes us to grow, and it brings us into maturity and spiritual adulthood.

The Word Declares the End from the Beginning

Then there is something else about the Word of God. We have here in this incredible Bible of 66 books the end described from the beginning. In other words, sometimes if we want to know whether a book is worth reading we often go to the last chapter and read it. The Bible is incredible because it tells you the end from the beginning. We find this again in Isaiah:

> *Remember the former things of old: for I am God, and there is none else; I am God, and there is none like me; declaring the end from the beginning, and from ancient times things that are not yet done; saying, My counsel shall stand, and I will perform all my pleasure (46:9–10).*

In this amazing Book you have everything. Here we are thousands of years later after dear Isaiah spoke these words by the Spirit of God, and we are actually in the beginning of a time that is described in the Word of God. It is all there, everything, right down to the last detail. And the most wonderful thing is that the Bible ends with the New Jerusalem coming down out of heaven, having the glory of God, a new heaven and earth, and we hear Jesus saying: Behold, I make all things new (Revelation 21:5). It is wonderful.

The apostle Peter says: "We have the word of prophecy (that is the prophetic Word of God) made more sure, whereunto ye do well that ye take heed, as unto a lamp shining in a dark place" (II Peter 1:19a). So this Word of God is a tremendous comfort to us.

The Sovereign Authority and Power of God

I want to say something about the sovereign authority, power, and the almightiness of God. It is one thing to have the Word of God, but it is the Word of God. We also need to understand the sovereign authority and power of God. Why should we be afraid of people like Ahmadinejad? or Adolph Hitler? or Lenin? or Stalin? or Mao Tse Tung? Why should we be afraid and quake over people like these? It is all here in the Book: "Behold, the Lord God will come as a mighty one, and his arm will rule for him: Behold, his reward is with him, and his recompense before him." And then this mighty One who seems to be a man of war says that He will lead His sheep. I think it is so beautiful that the whole tone changes. "He will feed his flock like a shepherd, he will gather the lambs in his arm, and carry them in his bosom, and will gently lead those that have their young" (Isaiah 40:10–11).

In the midst of all this turmoil and conflict, you have this amazing promise that the sovereign power of God and the almightiness of God is for His own. It is for the fulfillment of His purpose and for the salvation of the unsaved. I find that tremendous.

There is None Equal to God

Beginning with verse 12 the Lord inquires:

Who hath measured the waters in the hollow of his hand, and meted out heaven with the span, and comprehended the dust of the earth in a measure, and weighed the mountains in scales, and the hills in a balance? Who hath directed the Spirit of the Lord, or being his counselor hath taught him? With whom took he counsel, and who instructed him, and taught him in the path of justice, and taught him knowledge, and showed to him the way of understanding? (Isaiah 40:12-14)

Has anyone else done this? Who did this?

Then He says in verse 15: "Behold the nations are as a drop of a bucket, and are accounted as the small dust of the balance: behold, he taketh up the isles as a very little thing." I love it. Everyone gets so afraid of all these Islamic nations and Iran with its nuclear program and everything else going on, but the Lord says, "They are just a drop in the bucket. They are fine dust, that is all. Do not worry about them." Are we going to worry about them? No, not if we are joined to the One who is Almighty. This mighty

One is going to carry the lambs in His bosom. There could not be a more tender picture. He is going to lead his flock.

The Lord Jesus said, "Fear not, little flock; it is the Father's good pleasure to give you the kingdom" (see Luke 12:32). How amazing is that?

Is there anyone equal to God? We know the simple answer to that. "Who will you liken Me to?" (See Isaiah 40:18a). Is there anyone else like Him? Have you realized how amazing it is that you have been saved? Do we really know what has happened to us? The Holy Spirit has not only opened our eyes, but He has positioned us in Christ. That is why the Lord Jesus put it so simply: "Abide in me, and I in you" (John 15:4a). But there is something even more wonderful. The Holy Spirit has opened our eyes, positioned us in the Messiah and made us one with the Father; therefore, all the sovereign power and authority of God the Father is ours. It will surround us; it will be for us. It is like the pillar of cloud and the pillar of fire. It will come between us and the enemy. It will shade us from the heat of the sun which can be devastating. It will be warmth in the cold of the night and a light in the darkness. Are you experiencing the Lord leading you and being with you in this way? Do you know in reality His coming between you and the enemy? Is it not wonderful?

The Nations are Like Grasshoppers in the Lord's View

The Lord will be absolutely faithful to His purpose. I love it here where He says: "He sits above the circle of the earth." Then He says: "The nations are like grasshoppers" (see Isaiah 40:22a). Now a grasshopper—poor creature—is the easiest thing to kill.

You can damage it in less than a second. When these huge things happened such as Nazism or Marxism, or these demonized leaders took power, who seemed so powerful, so eternal, so immoveable, so invincible, we hear the Lord saying: "They are grasshoppers." That is from the Lord's view. (Not always from our view, I am afraid). Then He goes on to say: "I can remove all these people in power. They are only there by my grace; therefore, I can remove them any time I want to" (see vv. 23–24).

We are told that they tried to kill Hitler long before He died, but they could not do it. They tried to kill Mao Tse Tung–they could not do it. In His strange wisdom God allows even dictators, tyrants and demonized men to rule. He brings them to power and He is the one who takes them down. You cannot live beyond a single moment that He has decreed. That is why I am not so bothered about Ahmadinejad because when the Lord says, "You have had it," he will fall from power—nuclear programs and devices or no nuclear programs and devices. There are his continual threats to Israel and the world. Do not think for a moment it is only Israel; he also hates the United States. I am not sure that your President understands that but he hates the United States, and if he has got a nuclear device for Israel, in the end, he will surely have a nuclear device for some of the Western nations as well.

God is Faithful to His Purpose

But why should we be afraid? God is faithful to His purpose. The Lord Jesus is going to return on time. I have no doubt about it, and it is thrilling to think about that. His purpose is going to be fulfilled in the saving of Israel. What a day that will be when the eyes of the Jewish people are opened, just like ours have been opened. And they will see Jesus and understand that this is the key to Jewish history—all their suffering, all the hatred of them and the determination of evil forces to destroy them. They will see in a single moment of time that Jesus is the key to Jewish history, Jewish suffering, and to Jewish destiny. Those natural branches have to be re-engrafted to the olive tree. You are in the olive tree by living faith given to you by God. You are wild olive branches, as I always say, some more wild than others! But thank God for the amazing grace with which He takes wild olive branches and grafts them into the good olive tree. The extraordinary thing is that He puts a wild olive branch into the good natural olive tree, and the wild branches bear fruit. That is against nature; it is contrary to nature. They take a wild trunk with its roots and then graft in natural branches, and they bear fruit. But for the Lord to take wild olive branches and graft them into a good olive tree and they bear fruit is incredible. But the purpose of God in the end is to save Israel. I do not know whether that means every single Jew that exists; it could mean all the elect, whatever that might mean in the end. But the wonderful thing is that this is the purpose of God, and He is absolutely faithful to fulfill it. So do not be afraid.

I personally believe that Islam is growing in power and is destined to nearly take the whole world. The money that is now in the hands of Islam is incredible. There is not a stock exchange in Europe that would not collapse if the money of Saudi Arabia and the oil sheikdoms was withdrawn. It is frightening. You see it in all the world media—BBC World Service, CNN World Service, and the other services. They have put so much money into it that now you have Muslim anchor men and women, Muslim programs, and other things. There is no need to be afraid, for God will use little Israel to break the back of Islamic power. They will come against her in force and the whole world will hold its breath. It will seem to be the final end of Israel and the final solution to the problem; but it will turn out quite the opposite. God will use our little people—seven and a half million in a postage stamp of territory in the Middle East—to break the back of Islam. I do not know how but I am convinced He will do it.

Furthermore, there are still numbers of Gentiles yet to be saved from all over the world, but when the full number of them are saved, then God will turn back to Israel and thus all Israel will be saved. I think that means everyone in the good olive tree, whether it is a wild olive branch or a natural olive branch—all of us will be in the same olive tree.

Birth Pangs of the Kingdom

Jesus spoke of this time as the birth pangs of the kingdom. Now birth pangs are not normally a joyful time. Of course, I have not experienced birth pangs, but I know from observation and from those who have told me that birth pangs are birth pangs. Now is it not interesting that Jesus spoke of this period that we are entering as the birth pangs of the kingdom? And then he also spoke of it as the *sorrows* of the kingdom (see Matthew 24:8). We are right there, but He is going to achieve His purpose. The point is that something is going to be born. That is the point of the birth pangs.

The Lord is not tired, He is not weary, He is not having fainting fits, and He has not retired. Many people seem to think that in the 21st century God has finally retired. He is vegetating somewhere in heaven because it is too much for Him. He has virtually exhausted Himself in the creation of the universe and this planet, and then when Adam and Eve fell, it wearied Him more. He worked out the plan of salvation which exhausted Him even more, and now, stressed and pressurized by all the evil that there is in the world, He has retired. But God has not retired; He is very much alive. And the wonderful thing is that all His power and strength and wisdom and life are available to us.

A Nation Is Great When It Is Faithful to the Word and Law of God

The Lord is able to give strength to the one who is on the point of collapsing. We have no need to be afraid as if the Lord is being taken by surprise at what is happening. He looks on the United States—the whittling down of the Constitution, the gradual removal of everything that is evidence of the Word of God or of Christianity or of the gospel—He sees it all, and He is not the least bit afraid. They are grasshoppers, just a drop in the bucket. I know you naturally good Americans think of yourselves as the great superpower. The Lord does not. As far as He is concerned, you are a flea that can be easily extinguished and eradicated! Your greatness came through faithfulness. Those early refugees that came to this great continent had nothing. They had no money or very little that they could claim as their own, but they had one thing—they had the Lord. And they were faithful to the Lord. Out of that came the greatness of the United States.

Even when you got rid of the tea in Boston, which was a dreadful thing to do, the Lord did not mind. Austin Sparks used to say they still make tea in the States with the same ratio of tea to water as when they chucked the tea over into the Atlantic. It was a dreadful thing. But the Lord did not mind; your getting rid of the tea was nothing to Him. The fact is that you honored the Lord, you respected His law and His word, and His law was written into your Constitution. That is what made America great. She has been until now, a bulwark for the gospel, a bulwark for the Word of God; she has protected Christian minorities in Indonesia, in Pakistan, in all kinds of countries by her very presence; but all that is on the way out. You must not think that the greatness of the United States and her superpower status is forever.

I lived in Britain at the time when it was a great superpower. She had colonies all over the world; she had great areas everywhere that belonged to her that were called dominions. She had a navy that went all around the world as a policeman. I remember Alan Redpath speaking in Duke Street Baptist Church, gripping the pulpit, getting very hot and red on a Sunday morning and saying, "As surely as I stand here God will judge the British Empire and this United Kingdom for what she has done to the Jewish people. She will lose all her empire and colonies, and she will become offshore islands of Europe." I remember it very well because I was only thirteen. I saw people get up and walk out, but I thought they had luncheon appointments. The pastor had gone on a bit longer than usual and was rather heated, and they wanted to keep their appointments. But I found out afterwards that they were British patriots, and they could not believe a pastor could possibly say that God would judge Britain. And now this is what is happening to this great country of America.

This is stressful, pressurizing, and hard to take; nevertheless, we can go through it not merely as survivors but as overcomers by the grace and power of God. May the Lord use this word to help every one of us.

Shall we have a word of prayer:

Beloved Lord, these words are not so easy to speak, but we pray together that You would touch our hearts. We have a responsibility to You, and insofar as most of us are citizens of the United States, we have a grave responsibility for what is happening. Dear Lord, burden our hearts, speak directly to us. Help us to find the power and the strength and the wisdom and the life that we need to be not merely survivors but overcomers. And we ask it in the name of our Lord Jesus.

.

2.
Made Powerful in the Lord

Isaiah 40:12–15

Who hath measured the waters in the hollow of his hand, and meted out heaven with the span, and comprehended the dust of the earth in a measure, and weighed the mountains in scales, and the hills in a balance? Who hath directed the Spirit of the Lord, or being his counselor hath taught him? With whom took he counsel, and who instructed him, and taught him in the path of justice, and taught him knowledge, and showed to him the way of understanding?

Behold, the nations are as a drop of a bucket, and are accounted as the small dust of the balance: behold, he taketh up the isles as a very little thing.

Isaiah 40:18–31

To whom then will ye liken God? or what likeness will ye compare unto him? The image, a workman hath cast it, and the goldsmith overlayeth it with gold, and casteth for it silver chains. He that is too impoverished for such an oblation chooseth a tree that

---

*will not rot; he seeketh unto
him a skillful workman to
set up a graven image that
shall not be moved. Have
ye not known? have ye not
heard? hath it not been told
you from the beginning? have
ye not understood from the
foundations of the earth? It is
he that sitteth above the circle of
the earth, and the inhabitants
thereof are as grasshoppers; that
stretcheth out the heavens as a
curtain, and spreadeth them
out as a tent to dwell in; that
bringeth princes to nothing; that
maketh the judges of the earth
as vanity. Yea, they have not
been planted; yea, they have
not been sown; yea, their stock
hath not taken root in the earth:
moreover he bloweth upon
them, and they wither, and the
whirlwind taketh them away
as stubble. To whom then will
ye liken me, that I should be
equal to him? saith the Holy
One. Lift up your eyes on high,
and see who hath created these,
that bringeth out their host by
number; he calleth them all by
name; by the greatness of his
might, and for that he is strong
in power, not one is lacking.
Why sayest thou, O Jacob, and
speakest, O Israel, My way
is hid from the Lord, and the
justice due to me is passed away
from my God? Hast thou not
known? hast thou not heard?
The everlasting God, the Lord,
the Creator of the ends of the
earth, fainteth not, neither is
weary; there is no searching of
his understanding. He giveth
power to the faint; and to him
that hath no might he increaseth
strength. Even the youths shall
faint and be weary, and the
young men shall utterly fall;
but they that wait for the Lord
shall renew their strength; they
shall mount up with wings as
eagles; they shall run, and not*

be weary; they shall walk, and
not faint (40:18–31).

II Corinthians 12:7–10

*And by reason of the exceeding
greatness of the revelations,
that I should not be exalted
overmuch, there was given
to me a thorn in the flesh, a
messenger of Satan to buffet
me, that I should not be exalted
overmuch. Concerning this thing
I besought the Lord thrice, that
it might depart from me. And he
hath said unto me, My grace is
sufficient for thee: for my power
is made perfect in weakness.
Most gladly therefore will I
rather glory in my weaknesses,
that the power of Christ may
rest upon me. Wherefore I
take pleasure in weaknesses,
in injuries, in necessities, in
persecutions, in distresses, for
Christ's sake: for when I am
weak, then am I strong.*

II Corinthians 4:7–18

*But we have this treasure
in earthen vessels, that the
exceeding greatness of the power
may be of God, and not from
ourselves; we are pressed on
every side, yet not straitened;
perplexed, yet not unto despair;
pursued, yet not forsaken;
smitten down, yet not destroyed;
always bearing about in the
body the dying of Jesus, that
the life also of Jesus may be
manifested in our body. For we
who live are always delivered
unto death for Jesus' sake, that
the life also of Jesus may be
manifested in our mortal flesh.
So then death worketh in us, but
life in you. But having the same
spirit of faith, according to that
which is written, I believed, and
therefore did I speak; we also
believe, and therefore also we
speak; knowing that he that
raised up the Lord Jesus shall
raise us also with Jesus, and*

shall present us with you. For
all things are for your sakes,
that the grace, being multiplied
through the many, may cause
the thanksgiving to abound unto
the glory of God. Wherefore
we faint not; but though our
outward man is decaying, yet
our inward man is renewed day
by day. For our light affliction,
which is for the moment,
worketh for us more and more
exceedingly an eternal weight
of glory; while we look not at
the things which are seen, but
at the things which are not seen,
for the things which are seen are
temporal; but the things which
are not seen are eternal.

May we have a word of prayer:

*Beloved Lord we are thankful that again we can find You here.
We are gathering to You, Lord; we are not asking You to join us.
We are coming into Your presence, and we want You to speak to us.
We commit this whole time to You, declaring that Jesus is Lord over this
place and over this room. We thank You that every spirit of darkness
and demonic spirit is under the feet of our Lord Jesus. Through His
death it has all been brought to zero, to naught, and we thank You for
it. And, Lord, we want to ask You to grant us open eyes. Even though
many of these things we may have heard, open our eyes to see more
clearly so that it will do something in us as we see it. May it not just feed
our heads but meet us in our hearts. Lord, we need You, and we commit
ourselves to You, thanking You for the anointing which You have dearly
won for us at Calvary. Into that anointing now we stand by faith for*

the speaking and for the hearing, in the name of our Lord Jesus. Amen.

Isaiah, chapter 40, is an amazing chapter because it was written to help those who were in the faithful remnant in Israel. The country was beginning to backslide, and with the eye of faith Isaiah saw clearly that much was going to crystalize and die and become merely a tradition and religion. And this amazing chapter was for those who were among the faithful remnant who felt the stress of the way everything was going and the pressure of growing darkness and death. He speaks to comfort those in the light of the coming of the Messiah to be faithful, to remain faithful, and to know the Lord. And that is what you and I need. We are now in a turning point in history, whether we like it or not. Things are growing more troubled, more broken up, and more difficult to bear. On every side we see a turning away from Biblical principle, a rejection of the Bible, a rejection of the gospel and the Word of God.

This is extraordinary, especially when you recall that here in this country alone, apart from any other, that all those who came here to begin with were believers fleeing from terrible persecution in Europe. They came in order to preach the Word of God freely, to seek the Word of God for themselves, and through the Word to find the Lord. The Constitution that was put in place basically came out of the living faith of the early settlers and those that followed. Today, all that is going. It has reached such a pitch that, for instance, even the things to do with Christmas have been removed. It is like a landslide of unbelievable proportion. Where will it end? Will it get better?

Unless there is an enormous awakening in which millions of people are brought into a saving experience of the Lord Jesus, who are awakened by the gospel and begin to read and study the Word of God—such as the Reformation, the Quaker movement, the Moravians in Europe, the great evangelical awakening through the Wesley brothers and Whitfield, and many others— I do not think this downward spiraling will be halted.

I think the nations are basically under judgment, especially the Western nations, those we used to call the "homelands." The third world was deemed the mission field. These homelands are now the mission field. You get more morality and more ethic or goodness in the third world in many cases than you now get in Europe and even in North America.

This word from Isaiah is tremendous because he speaks of people fainting, having no strength, and being unable to face this downward spiral. It is a marvelous word to every one of us to hear. It is for us to remember: "He giveth power to the faint and increaseth strength to those who have no might" (see Isaiah 40:29). So there is hope in whatever conditions we might find ourselves and whatever we are moving into now. There is real hope for those who know the Lord and who seek Him.

The Promises of God are Yea and Amen

There is a glorious promise here that comes at the end of this prophecy:

They that wait for the Lord shall renew their strength; they shall mount up with wings as eagles; they shall run, and not be weary; they shall walk, and not faint (Isaiah 40:31).

Now the New Testament has a tremendous amount in it about running and receiving the prize. It is all there. And there is even more about walking the walk of faith, and how we are to do this. It is all in the New Testament. There is the promise that we can be overcomers; not just running and walking but we can be like eagles mounting up and up and up into the very presence and experience of our risen Lord.

This word "wait for the Lord" is a glorious promise. Will you please note that it is waiting for the Lord, not waiting on the Lord. Of course, it is very important to wait *on* the Lord, but it is even more important to wait *for* the Lord. To wait on the Lord, to serve Him or to patiently endure is tremendous. But even more important in these days into which we are moving is the waiting for the Lord. The Hebrew word has the feeling within it of not just waiting in this sense: "Oh, well, I am waiting; whether patiently or impatiently, I am waiting on the Lord until He calls or until He does something." The feeling of this word in Hebrew "*qavah*" is simply "to wait in certain hope." We are not waiting in a hope against hope that somehow something will happen; this is a waiting patiently in God-given hope. It is an expectation; it has the feeling of expectation. Some modern versions actually say that you wait expectantly, and that is the idea here. What a tremendous word this is that comes to us in the midst of fainting, having no might, and feeling the stress and pressure: "Those that wait *patiently, expectantly,* in *certain hope* for the Lord, *will* renew their strength. They *shall* run and not be weary; they *will* walk and not faint (see Isaiah 40:31).

Could the Lord be more gracious to us in giving a word like this? Do we believe it? Do we believe that in these days of economic stress, financial instability and climatic change—with more to come—that we can wait for the Lord in certain hope and experience a renewing of our strength?

They Shall Exchange Their Strength

Our dear brother Dr. F. B. Meyer used to say about this phrase—"they shall renew their strength"—the word means that they shall *exchange* their strength. Now I have looked everywhere trying to find in the Hebrew if it really does say exchange. However we do see it in some of the modern versions. Of course, this Book, whether it is modern or old is a translation and the thing we have to try and discover is what the original Hebrew, Aramaic or Greek say. This word in some of the versions is: *They shall gain new strength.* But it still does not quite get it. Dr. F.B. Meyer was not wrong when he sort of created a little commentary on it and said, "They shall exchange their strength." What did he mean? He said: "Their faintness, being without power, and without might, they will exchange for His power, might, and strength." Personally, I think that gets right to the heart of this promise. God's promise to us as believers in the last phase of world history, whatever it means and signifies and however long it will last, is a marvelous promise to every born again believer. They shall exchange their strength. For those who have fainted they shall do the impossible; they will mount up with wings as eagles. That is one thing you could not say is "fainting." To be able to take off from the ground without a run up and simply take off is certainly not a fainting fit. It is not indicative of someone who has no might or power. "They shall mount up with wings as eagles, they shall run and not be weary; they shall walk and not faint." Thus we have: "mount up with wings," "run," and "walk." It is not a description of someone who is fainting or laid out by the track, totally exhausted and finished. This is the description of someone who has exchanged their weakness for His power. I find this tremendous, and I cannot think of anything more wonderful. God's promises are marvelous.

When I was young, I was not very well at one point, and when I went to the doctor he gave me an examination and said, "I think you are all right, but I am going to prescribe a pill. Now this pill is the equivalent of a whole fruit shop, but I think it will do the trick." I could not believe that this one little pill could provide all the fruit I needed. I do believe in healing, but because I am so irrepressible and so impossible the Lord probably has to do this to keep me dependent upon Him. But the fact of the matter is that this one little pill did the trick—that I had all the oranges, the grapefruit, the mangoes, the papaya, the kiwi in one single little small pill. God's promises are pills.

When you take one of God's promises, you have the whole book from Genesis 1 to Revelation 22. It is all in the promises.

The Promises Enable us to Experience the Lord

Why does God give us the promises? "That we might become partakers of the divine nature" (see II Peter 1:4). Then again, He gives us these promises that we might experience the Lord and partake of Him. Jesus said, "I am the bread of life, and he that eateth My flesh and drinketh My blood ..." (see John 6:54, 56).

It is amazing. We eat and drink to live physically; and thus it is with us in the spiritual. And it happens because we are given the promises of God, and when the Holy Spirit applies a promise to our condition, to our circumstances or to some problem we might have with a relationship, then incredibly it happens.

"For how many soever be the promises of God, in him is the yea: wherefore also through him is the Amen, unto the glory of God through us" (II Corinthians 1:20). It would take you a long time to study the whole Bible from Genesis to Revelation, but in one single promise everything that is in the Godhead is yours in reality and practice.

These glorious promises are something tremendous for us to stand upon and to know the Lord. In another passage in Isaiah He calls Himself "the everlasting God," "the Creator of the ends of the earth" (see Isaiah 40:28). This is truly mind blowing from one point of view, and even from theology it just knocks you out. Consider for a moment what this means—"the everlasting God."

I Am What You Need

When God appeared to Moses in the burning bush, He said to him: "You are to go to Egypt, speak to Pharaoh, and say: 'Let my people go.'" Never in his life did Moses think he was going to get a commission like that. He was eighty when he said to the Lord: "Excuse me, but who am I to say sent me when the Pharaoh says, 'Who are you? What have you come about?'" And the Lord said, "I AM that I AM. Tell them I AM has sent you." Now that is great material for theological seminaries and Bible schools. But I remember a little Irish evangelist who came to Halford

House quite regularly. He was a wonderful brother. He was not very tall and he was nearly as wide as he was tall. He actually used to put his little Bible on his stomach as a lectern and flip the pages over. He led my father, who was very aristocratic, to the Lord. It was unbelievable. He was a milkman in Dublin, and he could neither read nor write. He was a good Catholic, and when he heard that an Irish evangelist was coming, who was reported to be screamingly funny and always cracking the most dreadful jokes about the Pope, he decided to go and hear him. He got saved, and as a result of this he taught himself to read and write so that he could study the Word of God. He became an evangelist known all over the counties and provinces of Ireland. It is incredible the number of people that came to the Lord through him.

One Sunday morning at the breaking of bread he was asked to give a word, and it was "I AM that I AM." He said, "This name of the Lord has left me stone cold. I searched everywhere for the meaning of 'I AM that I AM.' I read this theological compendium and that theological compendium; I heard that He had no beginning and no end, that He was the Almighty; that His power was limitless, that His knowledge was without measure, that all wisdom was found in Him, that He was everywhere at the same time, and it still left me cold." I got on my knees and said, "I am sorry, Lord, but I do not understand Your name. I know the unmentionable name of God in Jewish circles is so important that it is not even spoken." And the Lord said to Him, "You do not understand My name? I AM everything you need. I AM a blank check, add what you will. Do you need power? I AM your power. Do you need grace? I AM your grace. Do you need salvation?

I AM your salvation. Do you need wisdom? I AM your wisdom. What do you need? I AM everything you need." That transformed Johnny Cochran's life. And I have to say that for me it was a shaft of light, shining on a very complex matter. Ever since then I have understood that this is the incredible relationship that God has with His redeemed. He says, "My name is Almighty; I AM eternal life, I AM the Savior of the world, I AM all wisdom, and I AM also everything you need. Whether it is at the level of the kitchen sink or your business or something to do with the nation or the nations, I AM what you need."

Now this is what the Lord is saying in Isaiah 40: "I am the everlasting God, the Creator of the ends of the earth. My understanding and my wisdom is inscrutable. You will never come to an end of it; it is forever beyond you." Then He says: "Those that wait for Him shall exchange their strength. They shall mount up with wings as eagles; they shall run, they shall walk."

How are we going to mount up with wings as eagles? Only, if I may put it reverently, by the great I AM. How are we going to walk and not be weary? By the great I AM. How are we going to walk and not faint in these conditions and these circumstances? Only by the great I Am. When God said that He was the everlasting God, the Creator of the ends of the earth, He was saying: "This covers everything. What is it that you really need? Do you need salvation? I AM your salvation." Now you may have been converted; you may have been baptized, your name may be on a church roll somewhere, but it becomes reality only when He becomes your salvation.

God is My Salvation

There is a wonderful little verse I often quote to myself: "Behold, God is my salvation; I will trust, and will not be afraid: for the Lord, even the Lord (that is the I AM), is my strength and my song; and he is become my salvation" (Isaiah 12:2). Thus you begin by saying, "God is my salvation," and you end by saying, "He has become my salvation." In other words, it is not just a conversion you had maybe twenty or forty years ago that has long since died and you are now a miserable, anemic Christian who literally finds it hard to sit in a meeting like this and listen. But somehow or other God has gotten into you, revived you, renewed you, and brought you into a living daily experience of Himself. He has become my salvation.

There is another wonderful Scripture that says, "God is unto us a God of deliverances; and unto Jehovah (that is the unmentionable name I AM) the Lord belongeth escape from death" (Psalm 68:20). God is unto us a God of deliverances. Do you need deliverance? It can be anything and everything, from the pet cat or dog to some relative who is destroying you. Here is the marvelous promise. God is salvation—all salvation, the fullness of salvation, complete salvation. It is nowhere else to be found. We will not find it in psychology or psychiatry or in some Eastern religion; it is in God Himself. And if you are born of God, here is the promise: if you wait for Him expectantly, you will exchange your strength for His; He will become your strength and power.

God is Absolute Power

Here is the second thing about God. He is almighty power, sovereign power, absolute power. They talk about nuclear power as if it is something tremendous but it is nothing compared with God. Such power! We have fainting fits, feel weak, stressed out, and the Lord says: "There is all the power you need—in Me. If you would only learn to wait on Me and wait for Me, you would discover the power." It is a never-ending fount and source of power. It is Almighty. With God nothing is impossible; nothing is too difficult; nothing is too hard. It is tremendous.

Do you need life? I know Paul said that Christian meetings should be arousing jealousy amongst the Jews, but truthfully, many Christian meetings would not arouse jealousy in a mouse; they are so boring. But what a tremendous thing it is when we have life, when a number of people come together and every one of them have had an experience of eternal life. God is eternal life. Jesus said: "I am the way, the truth, and the life. I am the resurrection and the life." In these days of departure from the Lord, of decay and deterioration, the growing strength on the part of Islam and other things, what a tremendous thing it is to find the Lord as eternal life, ever fresh and ever flowing.

Rivers of Living Water

Jesus once said, "He that believeth on me (that is, *into* me); He that believeth into me, from within him shall flow out rivers of living water" (see John 7:38). There is a place in the Himalayas where four or five of the greatest rivers in the world have their source, all within a few square miles—the Irrawaddy in Bangladesh, the Ganges, the Yangtze Jiang, the Mekong and others. Do you know that when the Lord Jesus becomes eternal life in you—you are believing into Him and experiencing Him—that from within you there are rivers of living water flowing out? Now I live in the Middle East, and it is incredible what water does here. Wherever water touches the desert, it becomes like a jungle—so green, fertile, and fruitful. Would it not be wonderful if every believer in the Lord became a source of not just a river, but *rivers* of living water? Can you imagine the number of unsaved people, unsaved families, unsaved relatives or unsaved business colleagues that would be touched? What a tremendous thing this would be; but it is all to do with waiting *for* the Lord. If we wait expectantly in certain hope for Him, then we have this promise. We will renew our strength, we will exchange our strength, and for our weakness will come His life and power.

If You Lack Wisdom

I might mention this matter of wisdom, which most of us lack; I certainly do. When I was first saved, Mrs. Andre, a Swedish lady who was a millionaire and lived around the corner from my family home, "adopted" me and my sister, in a sense. She decided that we came from a totally unsaved family with no knowledge of God or the Bible and when my sister and I were saved, she took care of us. I learned so many things from her, but she always used to say to me: "Now Lance, you are a very arrogant young man, and you lack wisdom. You do not have the kind of wisdom that you need." She said, "There is a promise for you in James:

'But if any of you lacketh wisdom, let him ask of God, who giveth to all liberally and upbraideth not; and it shall be given him'" (1:5). Somehow it sank into my heart, and every day for years I said to the Lord: "I do not have any wisdom." I was still arrogant and said what I thought, which was not so good at times, but I still prayed every morning: "Lord, I have no wisdom. Please, will You give me wisdom?" If I have any understanding of the Word of God or of the Lord, I think it has come from that simple standing on the promise that Auntie Dagmar said to me all those years ago.

Whatever comes our way, everything that you and I need for endurance is in Him, and He can be exactly what we need. Remember the fire in the old thorn bush? This is exactly the same. There was no power, no ability, no life, no wisdom in that thorn bush, but the fire in it burned and burned, and the bush was not consumed. God was saying to Moses: "This thorn bush is you. It has taken Me eighty years to bring you to this place. You are the bush, I am the fire. When I—the fire—get into the bush, history is made, and the will and purpose of God is fulfilled. Thus it is with every one of us; however insignificant we may feel, when the fire gets into us, then the purpose of God begins to be fulfilled.

He Is in Us as Power and Strength

The ability to endure is an amazing thing. When we are young we are full of hope and think we are full of ability. We think we can do it and much else, but after a while we get knocked around by the world and we begin to go down. Then we begin to faint because we are powerless. That is when the Lord comes and says: "I am the everlasting God, the Creator of the ends of the world, and there is no end to My wisdom and understanding. Those that wait for Me shall exchange their strength."

The word says here: "He gives power to those who are fainting and He increaseth strength to those who have no might" (Isaiah 40:29). Now I do not know if that gets you into the category. I think it gets me into it. What a wonderful promise this is! He will be our power and our strength. I cannot think of anything more gracious and more wonderful for us as we face all that we are moving into. He keeps His word—He increases strength when we have no might; He gives power when we are fainting.

Paul's Stake in the Flesh

I consider Paul the greatest apostle, and I am sick to death when I hear in many Messianic circles the way they downgrade him as if he is nothing, as if he is the architect of Christianity, and that if we had only kept with what Jesus said we would be safe. I think it is a lot of nonsense. Paul is the greatest of the Jewish sages, and the greatest rabbi of them all. He surpasses everyone in his understanding of the gospel and his understanding of the counsel of God. He says in II Corinthians: "Because of the exceeding greatness of the revelations given to me God gave me a messenger of Satan, a thorn in the flesh" (see 12:7). Conybeare and Howson, those incredible academics and masters of Greek, translated it like this: "It was not a thorn in the flesh, but a stake in the flesh." It was not a little prick somewhere in his body, on his foot or arm or hand, but something that impaled him. We could almost say that it crucified him. He called it a messenger of Satan. I always remember C.T. Studd and the way he used to upset the evangelical world to no end all the time. Because he came from such an aristocratic family, he could not care less and used to say exactly what the truth was. He wrote that parody on the hymn—"Onward Christian Soldiers! Marching as to war"— this way: "Backward Chocolate Soldiers! Marching as from war, with the candy floss before you, going on before." That upset the whole evangelical world. How could he take a sacred hymn like that and change it? But he said, "They are not Christian soldiers, and they are not marching as to war."

Dear old C.T. Studd said another thing that also upset them. I hardly dare say it for fear that some of you will get angry with me, but he said on one occasion: "Satan is the greatest servant God has because everything he does, God turns to blessing." When he crucified the Lord Jesus and thought he had won, it was the salvation of the world. And if you look back in your life, you will find that every terrible thing that you could call a messenger of Satan has turned out to bring you into a deeper understanding of the Lord and His ways, into a real experience of His grace.

To say that the apostle Paul had been given a messenger from Satan is really terrible. Who gave this messenger of Satan to Paul? Obviously it was the Lord God Himself. He did it to keep Paul— the irrepressible Paul—broken and humble. And so he wrote these extraordinary words in his second letter to the Corinthians which is probably the most personal of all the letters he ever wrote. He said: "Most gladly therefore will I rather glory in my weakness that the power of Christ may rest (or in Greek, tabernacle) upon me" (chapter 12:9). That word "tabernacle" is an amazing word to us because it was the dwelling place of God. Therefore, what he was really saying was that these weaknesses of his had caused God to be his dwelling place. He besought the Lord three times to remove the thorn. I wonder how many more times he asked the Lord after this letter was written; but we do not know. What we do know is that the Lord said to the apostle Paul: "My grace is sufficient for thee." Here was a messenger of Satan, a stake in his flesh, but: "My grace is sufficient." Then the apostle understood it and said, "When I am weak, then I am strong. When I am most broken, the Lord is most whole. When I am down, the Lord can use it and me."

This is incredible! You may consider this to be some form of dark, heavy holiness: "Oh, dear, we are all to dress in black, never smile, and never laugh because we must all be broken." No, you will never do it. Do not think you can crucify yourselves or that you can break yourselves; it is impossible. The strength of our self-life is so strong that no one can break it. We can go up on a pillar and sit on it as they did in the early days of Christianity and nearly wither to death in the sun—like the Hindus do—but it will not do anything. You can wear horse-hair shirts or those great collars they used to wear in monasteries with spikes all round them, which clamped upon you and caused blood to actually flow, and it will not do anything. This affliction to the flesh will avail nothing.

I Can Do All Things in Him

Do not worry your little head. God will send you enough problems, afflictions, and tribulations to bring you to the place of fainting and no strength; then for the first time, when you know you have no wisdom, you have no strength or power and very little life, then you will take the quantum step of faith. "I can do all things in him that strengtheneth me" (Philippians 4:13). But you can only say that when you have come to the place where you can do nothing. Then you will be able to take this step of faith: "I can do all things in him (that is, in the Messiah) that strengthens me." He gives power to the faint, and to those who have no might, He increases strength. It is incredible, it is colossal, it is wonderful.

Some will say, "That is not the Christian life; the Christian life is joy and peace and hilarity. What a miserable kind of gospel you are preaching." I can only say it is Pauline. What Paul said was very simple: "When I came to the place that I was broken and had no power and was fainting, the Lord said: 'My grace is sufficient for thee.'" "Sufficient? Lord, surely You could help by taking away the stake. Surely You could help by removing the messenger of Satan." "No," the Lord said, "that is the thing that will bring you to my grace—grace sufficient."

Now I have to tell you that by nature I am a whiner. I find myself all the time whining to the Lord: "Help me, Lord, help me." Everything has to be, "Oh, help me Lord." I am a real whiner. Because of this, now and again the Lord has to break through my whining and say, "Why do you not try this: I can do all things in Him who strengthens me?" It is another quantum step from: "I am hopeless and empty; I have no wisdom or power. Dear Lord, please come and help me; get behind me and support me." And the Lord is saying, "I am not going to do anything of the kind. You have to learn to take that step of faith: I can do all things in Him who strengthens me." "All things" means all things. How do we do it? In Him who strengthens us. Where are we? We are in

Christ. We are joined to Christ. The everlasting God is ours in Christ. The Creator of the ends of the earth is ours in Christ.

Treasure in Earthen Vessels

The apostle Paul says in II Corinthians this marvelous statement: "We have this treasure in earthen vessels" (4:7a). Can you believe that God would ever put priceless eternal treasure in little clay pots? They are so fragile that if you drop them they will break. They are not china, not even porcelain, but clay, earthenware, terra cotta. Only God could take priceless treasure and put it into an earthen vessel. Then He begins to explain what He means, and I have to say, it is a bit of a shock. If someone stood up and gave their testimony as a Christian and said, "I am perplexed, I am straightened, I am knocked down, and I am pursued all the time," we would say this man or woman is a candidate for deliverance. Let us send this person to some ministry that can help them. But the apostle Paul said exactly that. He says, "We are pressed on every side," (there is the stress), "perplexed," (we send people to Bible school so that they are not perplexed). He is always pressed on every side, perplexed, and pursued, which means the enemy is on our tail all the time. Do you feel it?

Then he says, "Smitten down, always bearing about in the body the dying of Jesus that the life also of Jesus may be manifested." As we read this catalogue we suddenly discover that there is a positive side to it. We are perplexed, yet not to despair. We are stressed, but it does not finish us. We are pursued, yet not forsaken. I think it was Canon Phillips, in his translation of these words, that put it like this: "smitten down, knocked down, but not knocked out." "Always bearing about in the body the dying of Jesus that the life also of Jesus might be manifested in our mortal body" (II Corinthians 4:10). That means our bodies can be filled with divine life. This brings us right back to this wonderful word that we are considering: "Those that wait for me shall exchange their strength. They shall mount up, they shall run, they shall walk; and weariness and fainting is gone."

Made Powerful in the Lord

The apostle said again in the Ephesian letter:

> *Be made powerful in the Lord, and in the strength of His might. Put on the whole armor of God, that ye may be able to stand against the wiles of the devil (6:10–11).*

Your version says, Be strong in the Lord, and this is not a false translation, but the Greek actually is nearer, "made powerful" in the Lord. It is not that you become strong; it is that *He* makes you strong, *He* makes you powerful. "Be made powerful in the Lord and in the strength of His might." It is all ours in Christ.

Put on the Whole Armor of God

Then it says, "Put on the whole armor." What is the armor? The armor is the Lord Jesus. There is only one way to walk in the darkness that is coming and that is in the armor of God—clothed with the Lord Jesus. That is why the Lord Jesus says, "Abide in me and I in you." That is the key. It goes on to say, "That ye may be able to withstand in the evil day, and, having done all, to stand. Stand therefore..." (Ephesians 6:13b–14a). The whole armor of God, which Paul describes, is simply Jesus. He is the helmet of salvation, the shield of faith, the loins gird about with truth, the feet shod with the gospel of peace—Jesus is everything. In Romans the apostle Paul puts it another very simple way: "Put ye on the Lord Jesus Christ, and make not provision for the flesh" (13:14a).

Putting on the whole armor of God is the key. You do not put on armor to go to a banquet or celebration or a party. To put on armor means you are in a war and the only way you are safe and secure is being in that gear which God has provided for you. May He make this real to every single one of us.

Shall we pray.

Beloved Lord, we pray that You will make this word real to us. We are in a turning point in history. We are not quite sure all that we are moving into and what it completely signifies; all we do know, Lord, is that You are sufficient; Your grace is sufficient. You have given us the armor that we need. And You have given us everything else. May it become our experience that as we wait expectantly in certain hope for the Lord we shall exchange our strength and mount up with wings as eagles, run and walk. We ask it in the name of Jesus; Amen.

3.
Mount up with Wings as Eagles

Isaiah 40:18–31

To whom then will ye liken God? or what likeness will ye compare unto him? The image, u workman hath cast it, and the goldsmith overlayeth it with gold, and casteth for it silver chains. He that is too impoverished for such an oblation chooseth a tree that will not rot; he seeketh unto him a skillful workman to set up a graven image, that shall not be moved. Have ye not known? have ye not heard? hath it not been told you from the beginning? have ye not understood from the foundations of the earth? It is he that sitteth above the circle of the earth, and the inhabitants thereof are as grasshoppers; that stretcheth out the heavens as a curtain, and spreadeth them out as a tent to dwell in; that bringeth princes to nothing; that maketh the judges of the earth as vanity. Yea, they have not been planted; yea, they have not been sown; yea, their stock hath not taken root in the earth: moreover he bloweth upon them, and they wither, and the whirlwind taketh them away as stubble. To whom then will ye liken me, that I should be equal to him? saith the Holy One. Lift up your eyes on high, and see who hath created these, that bringeth out their host by number; he calleth them all by name; by the greatness of his might, and for that he is strong in power, not one is lacking.

Why sayest thou, O Jacob, and speakest, O Israel, My way is hid from the Lord, and the justice due to me is passed away from my God? Hast thou not known? hast thou not heard?

The everlasting God, the Lord, the Creator of the ends of the earth, fainteth not, neither is weary; there is no searching of his understanding. He giveth power to the faint; and to him that hath no might he increaseth strength. Even the youths shall faint and be weary, and the young men shall utterly fall: but they that wait for the Lord shall renew their strength; they shall mount up with wings as eagles; they shall run, and not be weary; they shall walk, and not faint.

May we have a word of prayer:

Beloved Lord, we are so thankful that we are here in Your presence and we always say, Lord—and we mean it—that when we are found in Your presence, anything can happen. With You nothing is impossible; nothing is too difficult or too hard. We praise You that at Your right hand, Father, the Lord Jesus sits, and into His hands You have committed all authority and power in heaven and on this fallen earth. We thank You, therefore, for Your almighty power and the eternal life which we have discovered as a living experience in our Lord Jesus. We pray that you will grant to us a spirit of wisdom and revelation in the knowledge of Yourself, that the eyes of our hearts may be enlightened, that we might know what is the hope of His calling, what is the glorious riches of His inheritance in the saints, and what is the exceeding greatness of His power toward us.

Lord, use this time, we pray. We are just ordinary, insignificant people; we are nothing in ourselves, and yet You have placed within us eternal treasure in giving us the Lord Jesus and His dwelling in us by the Holy Spirit. There is eternal treasure in every one of us. Open our eyes to see what is ours in the Lord Jesus as we move so quickly into turmoil, conflict, darkness, and the breakup of the society that we have known. Will You, Lord, speak to us to prepare us for these days that are coming upon the face of the earth? And will You in some way, Lord, challenge us? Hear our prayer. In Your death on Calvary You have won for us everything we could ever need to reach Your goal and Your glory.

Lord, please touch us now. For that we need the anointing, grace and power that You have won for us at Calvary, and You make it a living experience and reality in the person of the Holy Spirit. Now we stand by faith into that anointing grace and power for the speaker and for the hearer. Fill this time with Yourself and touch our hearts, and we shall be careful to give You all the praise and all the glory. We ask this in the name of our Messiah, the Lord Jesus. Amen.

We have been considering this amazing prophecy in Isaiah 40 as he looked down the corridors of time. He saw a time of silence when the Lord would not speak for 400 years and in that time there would be all kinds of movements—much backsliding on the part of Israel, a hardening, a kind of conception of the Messiah's coming that would somehow keep them from seeing Him when He came.

We considered the fact that the Word of our God liveth and abideth forever and about our being born of that Word. That is how alive this Bible is. When the Holy Spirit takes this Book and breathes it into us, we are born of God—just as we were born physically. Suddenly our eyes opened, we began to breathe, we began to eat, we began to drink, and before long we began to hear. Then we began to crawl and the nightmare came to our parents when we stood up for the first time and they had to watch us all the time. We grew, and whether we are old and white haired or young and full of life, it all came from that one foot of flesh when we were born. The apostle Peter says in his first letter that we are born again of the living Word of God (see 1:3). This Word of God is: "Living and active and sharper than any two edged sword, dividing between soul and spirit" (see Hebrews 4:12a). It is amazing!

We have also considered the almighty power of God. I am not a scientist, not even remotely one. I have always been on the more artistic and poetic side of things and my studies were all to do with classical and modern Chinese Mandarin. Therefore, I cannot dazzle your brains with the Milky Way and light traveling around the earth and all those galaxies in space which are wonderful things. Nevertheless, they are peanuts as far as God is concerned. He is infinitely powerful, infinitely glorious, and infinitely living. He never dies, He never grows weary, and He never has to lie down like I do now for a little siesta. God never has a siesta;

He does not need it. He is always alive, always listening, always there, and always at hand. When the Scripture says that the Lord is at hand, look at your hand; that is how far away He is. But He is even nearer than that. He lives within you, if you are born of God.

This infinite power, the almightiness of power is ours in Christ. In this amazing chapter the Lord takes all these verses and says, "Who will you liken Me to? Who is My equal?" And then you suddenly discover that this almighty One is a shepherd and He leads His sheep. He takes up the lambs and holds them to His bosom, and He gently leads those with young. The almightiness of God and the tenderness and sensitivity of God are a remarkable combination. Mercy and truth have kissed each other—love and righteousness in One. And all this is available to us. I find it amazing!

The Faithful Remnant

We also are at a turning point in history like that dear remnant of the faithful in the nation of Israel before the Messiah was born—the shepherds, the kings, (we call them kings but we are not sure; they were wise men that came from far), Zacharias and Elizabeth. There was also Simeon who took up the Lord in his arms and said, "Now let Your servant depart in peace for mine eyes have seen Your glory; I have seen the Messiah, a light for the Gentiles and the glory of Your people Israel" (see Luke 2:29–32). And then there was Anna who was so faithful, and others who are not named. This is the remnant of the faithful, and these are the ones to whom Isaiah spoke: "Do not be stressed by the backsliding of the nation; do not be stressed by the tradition or institutional religion that has now become the norm. The Lord, the everlasting God, the Creator of the ends of the earth is yours, and all His power and word is yours." He has actually defined the end from the beginning. In other words, we are not just left in a terrible world in which demonic power seems to be all powerful. He has already told us what to expect and given us the fact that all the grace and power of God will be available to us in those days.

All for the Lord—or Nothing

Not one person will survive in these days that are coming upon us unless we learn how to appropriate the grace and power of Christ. Now I know immediately some will say, "Ah, but we are going to be raptured." Thank God, I personally believe in the rapture; but let us not make it a form of escapism. It is perfectly clear from the Word of God that we are to go quite a way into the days of Antichrist before the rapture takes place. I have never been able to understand Western Christians when they say, "We are going to be raptured and taken away; therefore, we do not have to worry ourselves about these things. Everything is going to pot and breaking down everywhere; why should we bother because the Lord is going to take us." First of all, I am not sure that the Lord is going to take every believer if they are lukewarm. After all, He said to the church of Laodicea: "I will vomit you out of My mouth" (see Revelation 3:16). I think the Lord will take those who are ready and the rest will go through the tribulation and be purified. In the old English the words are much more beautiful: "I will spew you out of my mouth" which sounds much kinder and more pleasant. But in the Greek it is translated as: "You make me sick." In essence what He is saying is this: "Because you are neither hot nor cold—you are in between and you are nothing—I get nauseated over you. You make me sick and I will vomit you out of my mouth." But this does not mean He is finished with us because in the days that come we will either have to be all for the Lord or nothing. There will be no neutral ground.

We see on every side that in the so-called Christian nations there is a terrible downturn. It is not in the States and the United Kingdom alone, but it is in every so-called Christian nation of Europe. Their national constitutions which came out of the Word of God and the law of God are being thrown on one side, contradicted, and changed in the interest of being modern and contemporary and keeping abreast with history. Do you not think that this will warrant judgment? Do you think that a nation, whose greatness has been solely due to God, when those people forsake Him, He will not judge that nation? We see this happening in Britain, in Germany, in the Netherlands, in the Scandinavian nations, in the Mediterranean nations; and what about the United States? There have been the worst fires, the worst floods, and the worst tornadoes in the not-so-long history of this nation, and still no one wakes up. What does that mean? It simply means that when God judges, He waits to see if there will be any repentance and any change of mind and heart. If there is none, further judgment comes. Then He waits. God is incredibly merciful. He does not love judgment as some people imagine and portray, as if He is some dreadful God that somehow loves to crush people, wound them, break them down and throw them forever into fire. The Lord will do anything to save from judgment. We see it in Egypt with the ten plagues. At times the Pharaoh's heart slightly wavered, but then he hardened it until in the end the judgment became catastrophic with the death of the firstborn, not only of every single family in Egypt including the royal family, but all the cattle (see Exodus 12:29).

Birth Pangs of the Coming Kingdom

I really fear for what is happening. We are in one of the great turning points of history. The Word of God is very clear about these days. The Lord Jesus spoke of it when He said: "In the end there will be signs in sun and moon and stars, and on the earth there will be distress, men's hearts failing them for fear and expectation of the things coming upon the face of the earth" (see Luke 21: 25–26). In another place the Lord Jesus spoke of these days into which we are moving as the birth pangs of the coming kingdom—labor pains (see Matthew 24:8). In some places it is translated as the "sorrows" of the coming kingdom. It is all in the Book. The Lord has given us the end from the beginning. And then He said: "My counsel shall stand and I shall perform all my pleasure" (see Isaiah 46:10b).

God's Ways for His People to Overcome

Now what are we to do? How are we to face this situation? Shall we, like ostriches, bury our heads in the sand and say, "I do not believe this; I think this is scare mongering. This is dreadful to have a speaker telling us all these awful things. That is not the gospel. The gospel is that we will be wafted into heaven on a bed of roses with the angels at our fingertips, doing everything we could possibly wish, saving us from all afflictions, all tribulations and all troubles of any kind until we see our Savior face to face." That is not the New Testament I know. People write to me from the updates I sometimes give and they are very angry. One brother said: "You need to see a psychiatrist." On another occasion a person wrote to me and said: "You know, it is dreadful the kind of things you are saying." I am imperturbable as far as these letters are concerned; but it is a very strange thing to me that in all the evangelical churches there has not been a word about the coming judgment. If that is not Laodicean, what is?

However, it does not matter if people say, "You always see the dark side of things and are putting out all these dreadful things that are going to happen." That is not my aim at all. It is to wake people up. Burying our head in the sand does not mean that these things will not happen; it just means that we think that by not looking at them and facing them, we will be happier. Some Christians tell me that the Old Testament is full of judgment and an angry wrathful God and the New Testament is full of grace and love and mercy. I want to tell you that the God revealed in the Old Covenant is as full of grace and mercy and love as the God Who reveals Himself in the New Testament. And the God who judges things in the Old, is the God who judges things in the New. The book of Revelation has the most fearful and horrendous accounts of judgment; so much so that many Christians will not read it. What are we to do? How are we to face this kind of situation? We find it at the end of this marvelous chapter:

Hast thou not known? hast thou not heard? The everlasting
God, the Lord, the Creator of the ends of the earth, fainteth not,

neither is weary; there is no searching of his understanding.
He giveth power to the faint; and to him that hath no might
he increaseth strength. Even the youths shall faint and be
weary, and the young men shall utterly fall: but they that
wait for the Lord shall renew their strength; they shall
mount up with wings as eagles; they shall run, and not be
weary; they shall walk, and not faint (Isaiah 40:28–31).

The Renewing of Our Strength

What a description of those shepherds. What a description
of those wise men who came from far. What a description of
Zacharias and Elizabeth and Simeon and Anna and the others,
whose names we do not even know. It is a wonderful description
of them. These words are for you and for me. All the almighty
power and life that is in the everlasting God—there He uses His
unmentionable, unspeakable name—and the Lord Jesus is ours.
He speaks of a time when those who are naturally virile, strong,
young, and agile, will faint, let alone we older ones; and then
comes this glorious promise.

They *shall renew their strength.* Now it is not waiting on
the Lord or waiting upon the Lord; it is waiting *for* the Lord.
In the Hebrew there is this wonderful idea of patient, expectant
hope in waiting for the Lord. *They shall renew their strength.*
As Doctor F.B. Meyer said, "They shall exchange their strength."
In other words, His strength will be their strength, His power will
be their power, His wisdom will be their wisdom, His life will
be their life. In the midst of all the trouble, turmoil and conflict,

they will have a testimony and bear the testimony of Jesus faithfully. That is a marvelous promise.

He Gives Us Wings to Mount Up

Then He says, "They shall mount up with wings as eagles." The eagle is created by God and fashioned in such a way that it can rise up by the air currents, higher and higher and higher; the currents are no barrier to it. God has created its feathers, the muscles of its wings and its body exactly for the conditions it will live in. The eagle nests in the most amazing and craggiest of places in the mountains. It is an incredible bird; whether you see it in America or in Israel it is the same. It is amazing. It bears its young up and tips them out of the nest in such craggy places. Can you believe the mother and father eagle will tip the babies out who are just little eaglets? Then it catches them with their wings, bears them up, and then, believe it or not, tips them over until they fall like a stone and then they discover they have wings They have muscles in the wings that have not yet been exercised. They have feathers, and now they suddenly discover why they have feathers. Thus they begin to fly.

The Lord Jesus Overcomes in Us

What an incredible picture this is of the overcomer. The whole of the New Testament speaks of overcomers. Hebrews 11 tells us of the overcomer all the way through history to that point of time. When the Lord Jesus spoke to the seven churches, to each one of them He said: "To him that overcomes, he that hath an ear, let him hear what the Spirit says to the churches" (see Revelation 2 and 3).

Overcoming is not an elitist idea. Sometimes people say, "Please do not talk about overcoming; it is sort of superiority, spiritual apartheid and racism. There are some believers who are super people and they are the elite. They rise to the top and the rest of us poor mortals are left below to wander as best we can." The Lord Jesus said in John's gospel: "These things have I spoken unto you, that in me ye may have peace. In the world ye have tribulation: but be of good cheer; I have overcome the world" (16:33).

When I was first saved as a lad of thirteen, reaching the bar mitzvah age, the Lord wonderfully saved me. I had never read the Bible and thought that Jesus was a whole lot of myths that had been thought up about Him. But when He saved me, nobody thought to ask if I had a Bible. I had never read the Bible. But somehow I got a little paperback Gospel of John, and I read it over and over again, until it literally fell to pieces. And then finally someone thought to give me a Bible.

When I first read this: "In Me you shall have peace, in the world you shall have tribulation, but be of good cheer, I have overcome the world", I thought to myself: "That is a mean thing to say. Why did the Lord say such a thing? 'I have overcome. You will have peace in Me, but in the world you will have tribulation; but be of good cheer I have overcome.'" It was not until much later in my life that I discovered that what the Lord Jesus simply meant was this: If you let Him as the Overcomer be your Lord, your Master, the King in your life—when you surrender your will to His will and you do not have your own agenda, but His agenda is your agenda—then in you He becomes the overcomer.

In American English there is a wonderful way of saying certain things that sound different from *English* English. The first time I ever came to the United States many years ago, I saw on the top of the *New York Times* this little statement: "English is the language which separates the United States from the United Kingdom." And there are a number of words you use which are pronounced a little different in English English. For example: we call the things in the sea that boats are anchored to *buoys* ("boys"). Of course, when you hear that, you think of a young lad; but you say booey. Now the amazing thing about the buoy is that it does not matter how rough the water is, the waves go over it and the thing disappears, but it always comes back out on top. When the Lord Jesus is residing in a human being—a saved, born-again being—and He has His way with that human being, then He is the means by which we always come out on top in every affliction and every period of suffering. No matter how difficult the circumstances are or a relationship is, by the grace of God we come out on top. This is the way we learn of Him throughout our lives.

They shall mount up with wings as eagles is an amazing promise. The eagle is built for high flying. He is built to be an overcomer. Who taught him to use the air currents? Those air currents could dash him against a rock, but he has learned by some inner wisdom how to use the air currents. Those air currents for you are circumstances, relationships, problems that are insoluble, difficulties that seem to be complex; they are the things that get you down. But if you have this kind of life in you, the Lord will use them to take you higher and higher and higher.

Four Examples of Ones Who Mounted up as Eagles

Fannie Crosby

I think of four ladies who learned to take the air currents and fly high as overcomers. One of them is Fannie Crosby. When she was a child, she had eye trouble; so they called in the doctor and he prescribed drops for her eyes. By mistake, he took acid instead of the drops and put them in her eyes, and Fannie Crosby's eyes were destroyed. She never saw again until she saw the Lord. But Fannie Crosby wrote hymn after hymn after hymn. She mounted up as an eagle with wings, higher and higher and higher.

Mary Slessor

Then I think of Mary Slessor. Mary Slessor was so afraid when the Lord called her to Calabar in West Africa. She was a Scotts woman from Edinburgh, and whenever she spoke, she was so afraid of men that she turned to the wall while she was speaking if they were present in the congregation because she could not face them. One wonders how in the world she was going to be a missionary. But she went to Calabar, and her heart was broken over the condition of twins; for in those days the people of the area when they had twins believed it was demonic, and they threw the babies as they were born out into the bush to be eaten by wild animals. And Mary Slessor would go out every night into the bush listening for the cries of babies. When she found them, she would bring them back with her, and through this she began a whole series of orphanages.

This woman was so extraordinary! In those days, these people hardly wore anything (we are talking about 200 years ago). There was a huge get-together of all the big African chiefs, and they sat there from sunrise for the whole day to try and work out a plan to bring peace to the tribes of the area. But they did not really want peace because they liked human flesh, and these wars between the tribes provided plenty of meat. They were cannibals. She sat there knitting while they all discussed, and every now and then the voices would rise and they would get angry. Then it would calm down a bit. But when it was near sunset, their voices had risen to a crescendo and she knew immediately that they had planned not to make an agreement. So she put her knitting down and walked around these men who hardly had on a feather or two to hide their nakedness, and boxed their ears one after the other. And they signed a peace treaty which lasted for 200 years, until the Biafra Rebellion. The Lord had given her a promise: "Kings and queens will bow before you," and when Queen Elizabeth went to Calabar, she went to Mary Slessor's grave and curtsied. Amazingly, the promise of God to Mary Slessor was fulfilled. She had mounted up with wings as eagles.

Amy Carmichael
Amy Carmichael came from Northern Ireland, but she felt called to India, and she went to the south of India. She upset the whole missionary community by writing a book, *Things as They Are*. They never spoke to her again. But she began a work in Southern India that became proverbial. She went into the temples to rescue children from temple prostitution. She rescued thousands of children, with helpers, of course.

Because the work had become so great, they wanted to expand it. There was another town nearby which had a place for sale, and they made an appointment to see it. They went by jeep over some seventy miles or so to this town, but the man who had the key was not there. Now in the tropics the dusk falls within a quarter of an hour, and as they waited for him to come, the dusk fell. Then he came with the key and opened the door. In respect they waited for Amy Carmichael—they called her "Amma"—to go first. No one knew that the coolies had dug a great deep trench just on the other side of the door, and in the dark Amma stepped forward and fell into this 9-foot deep ditch.

She broke her hip, her ankle, and her arm. They tenderly got her up, put her back in the jeep, and went as fast as they possibly could without making it more difficult for her, to the nearest hospital, which was about 100 miles away. When they got there, she was treated; but for Amy Carmichael one whole section and phase of her ministry was over, and her worldwide ministry was just beginning. She wrote a book while she was in the hospital entitled *Rose from Briar*. In the introduction she said, "I feel a cheat to speak to those of you who are suffering insoluble problems with your health. But I have learned so much in the six months that I have been on my back. I shall walk again and be able to go back to my work," (that is why I feel she said "a cheat") "but I have learned lessons and I feel that I must pass them on." She did not realize she would never walk again until the day she went to be with the Lord. But Amy Carmichael's books and her poems have gone all over the world. I have found the most extraordinary thing that the only books that have touched the spirit of people who have insoluble problems in health and other things to do with their health, were Amy Carmichael's. It was truly deep speaking unto deep. She was an overcomer, and she mounted up with wings as an eagle.

Mary Rees

Then I remember Mary Rees who took over for a while from C.T. Studd in the southern part of Congo. She was so fearful as a girl that she could not cross a field if a cow was in it, and then the Lord called her to the Congo of all places. She would travel around on C.T. Studd's bike that had those solid wheels. She was terrified of the baboons that began barking as soon as they saw her come out of her little hut and get on the bike. And she said, "They think I am a baboon because when I start cycling, they swing from tree to tree following me all the way as I go on my visits." One day she met one of the mountain gorillas sitting in the park, and she did not know what to do. She was terrified, and all her old fears came back. As she looked at this gorilla she thought: what am I to do? She turned her heart to the Lord and said, "Lord, give me wisdom. You have said that if we lack wisdom You will give it to us, and You will not investigate or interrogate. Please give me wisdom." And the Lord said to her: "Give him a tract." (Now the Lord did not mean by that He would convert the gorilla.) But she had tracts in French in the back of her bike, so she gingerly took one of these tracts out and went toward the gorilla and held it out to him, and the gorilla got up from sitting in the park, came across, and took it. And while he was looking at it this way and that way, she got on her bike and sped off. That is a smaller picture of being an eagle with wings.

Three Ways of Overcoming

They Shall Mount Up with Wings

Is not the word of God amazing? Do you remember when the Lord talked about the seed—the Word of God—falling into the ground and He said it would yield fruit, a hundred-fold, sixty-fold, and thirty-fold? (See Matthew 16:23.) Why did He put the highest thing first and then go down? Our natural instinct would be to say, thirty-fold, sixty-fold, a hundred-fold. No, the Lord said, "a hundred fold," as if that was the thing He was after. I wonder if the Lord is saying the same thing here. "They shall mount up with wings as eagles." And then they shall run, and then they shall walk. That is the first marvelous way of overcoming.

They Shall Run

The second is: *They shall run and not be weary.* It is not quite the same as rising up with wings as eagles; nevertheless, there is a great deal in Scripture about running and the prize to be won. There is the race that we are in, keeping our eyes on Jesus.

So in the midst of all this darkness, judgment of nations, and everything going wrong, the Lord says, "Do not let it stop you; you go straight on." Let the Lord do in your life what He has purposed to do. Do not let the conditions around you affect you. Be overcomers. Let the Lord in you be the overcomer. And if you cannot mount up with wings as eagles, at least you can run and not be weary. And if you cannot manage running, what about walking?

They Shall Walk

"They shall walk and not faint." What a tremendous amount there is in the Word of God about walking: "Walk worthily of your calling" (see Ephesians 4:1). "Walk in the light" (see I John 1:7). Walk in love (see Ephesians 5:2). "Walk by faith" (see II Corinthians 5:7). Walk in fellowship (see I John 1:7). You can say, "I am in a race but I am so weary. It is no good; I am just about exhausted." But if you remember the everlasting God, that the almightiness of His power is yours, you can run and not be weary. You can walk and not faint. We know that we should walk worthy of His calling but many of us faint. We are given to fainting fits; but we should not faint. We have a never-ending supply of the life, the grace, and the power of God in the Lord Jesus. The problem is to discover it. When the eyes of our hearts are opened, suddenly we realize it is ours in Christ.

The Headship of Christ

It is not only that we know what the hope of His calling is, and what the glorious riches of His inheritance in the saints is—not your inheritance but the Lord's inheritance in the saints—which is the church. Not only that, but there is the exceeding greatness of His power to us-ward who believe (see Ephesians 1:18–19). And then he gives the illustration:

Which He wrought in Christ, the Messiah Jesus, when he raised him from the dead, and made him to sit at his right hand in the heavenly places, far above all rule and authority, and power, and dominion, and every name that is named, not only in this world, but also in that which is to come (Ephesians 1:20–21).

Are we to have the exceeding power like that? Yes, we should have it. "That the exceeding greatness of His power..." And then he goes on and says: "And gave him to be head over all things to the church, which is his body" (vv. 22–23a). Think of it! Think how it would transform our prayer meetings, our times of intercession, if we understood that He has been made Head over all things—not a few things—all things to the church which is His body. Wonderful!

Seated in Heavenly Places

We are told in Ephesians 2 that we have been made to sit with Him in heavenly places (see v. 6). Is that just theology? Is it merely doctrine? Or is it a reality? I remember Mr. Sparks, when he was a young man, was greatly helped by Dr. F.B. Meyer. He made an appointment to see him over a problem he had, and when he got to Dr. Meyer's home, the house mistress opened the door and said, "The doctor is not here just yet, but he will be here shortly; please go into his study and sit down." He went into the study, and like any young man, he began to look around to see what the great man was reading and studying. He looked all round at the books and suddenly he was riveted by a little plaque on the mantel piece. On it, engraved in gilt, were the words: "Look Down." And he wondered what Dr. Meyer thought it meant. We have always been told in evangelical circles "Look up." At that moment Dr. Meyer came in, apologized for being late and said, "I see that you are transfixed by that little plaque on my mantel piece." "Yes," said Mr. Sparks, "should it not be look up?" And Dr. F.B. Meyer said, "It is all a question of our position. If we are seated with Christ, we will look down on everything, but if we are not seated with Christ, we must look up." What a help that can be when we are faced with the next problem. To be able to face it from the throne of the Lord with the wisdom of the Lord, with the life of the Lord, with the power and grace of the Lord, is in itself an answer to the problem. The problem may continue for a long time but our position will change us. In an amazing way we will come into a new and deeper experience of what it is to wait expectantly in certain hope for the Lord.

May the Lord bring home to all of us the need to know Him in a much deeper way than we have ever known Him before.

Shall we pray:

Beloved Lord, we lift our hearts to You. You know us, Lord; You know our condition, You know where we stand, and we need You. We need that You will open the eyes of our hearts to see just what You have done with us. Father, by the Holy Spirit You have positioned us in the Messiah, and in Him we discover the eternal life of the everlasting God. In Him we discover almighty, infinite power. In Him is total wisdom. All Your fullness, Father, is in the Lord Jesus, and we are made full in Him. Dear Lord, use this time to speak to our hearts, to strengthen us, to help us to face the days that are coming and to be overcomers. We ask it in the name of our Lord Jesus. Amen.

Other books by Lance Lambert

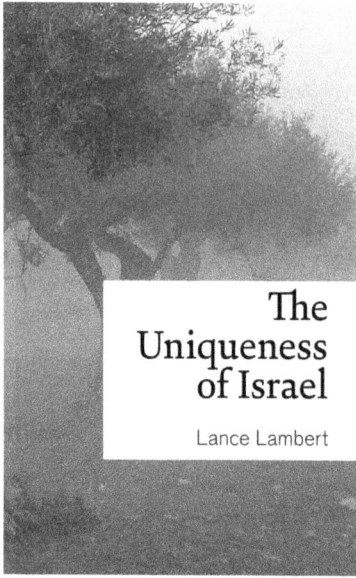

The Uniqueness of Israel

Woven into the fabric of Jewish existence there is an undeniable uniqueness. There is bitter controversy over the subject of Israel, but time itself will establish the truth about this nation's place in God's plan. For Lance Lambert, the Lord Jesus is the key that unlocks Jewish history He is the key not only to their fall, but also to their restoration. For in spite of the fact that they rejected Him, He has not rejected them.

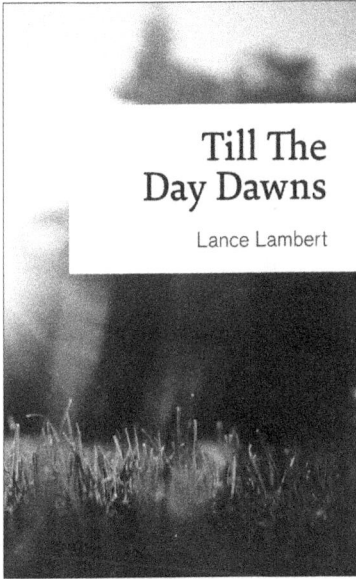

Till the Day Dawns

"And we have the word of prophecy made more sure; whereunto ye do well that ye take heed, as unto a lamp shining in a dark place, until the day dawn, and the day-star arise in your hearts." (II Peter 1:9).

The word of prophecy was not given that we might merely be comforted but that we would be prepared and made ready. Let us look into the Word of God together, searching out the prophecies, that the Day-Star arise in our hearts until the Day dawns.

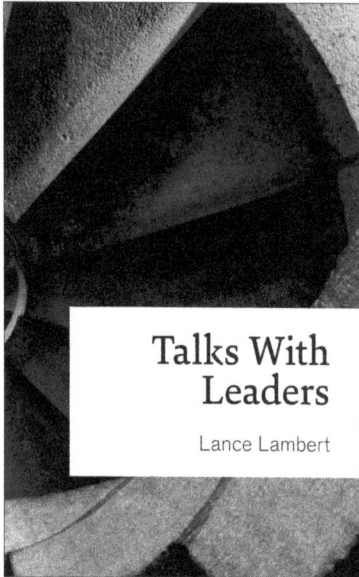

Talks With Leaders

"O Timothy, guard that which is committed unto thee ..."
(1 Timothy 6:20) Has God given you something? Has God
deposited something in you? Is there something of Himself
which He has given to you to contribute to the people of God?
Guard it. Guard that vision which He has given you. Guard that
understanding that He has so mercifully granted to you. Guard
that experience which He has given that it does not evaporate or
drain away or become a cause of pride. Guard that which the Lord
has given to you by the Holy Spirit. In these heart-to-heart talks
with leaders Lance Lambert covers such topics as the character
of God's servants, the way to serve, the importance of anointing,
and hearing God's voice. Let us consider together how to remain
faithful with what has been entrusted to us.

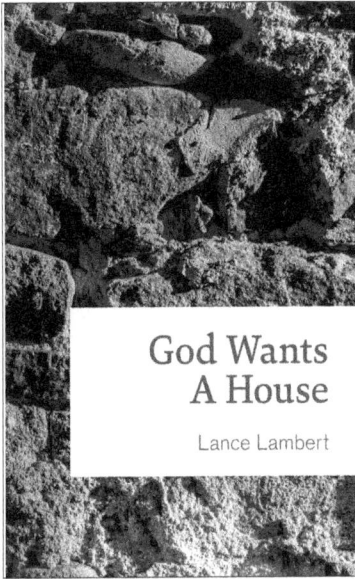

God Wants A House
Lance Lambert

God Wants a House

Where is God at home? Is He at home in Richmond, VA?
Is He at home in Washington? Is He at home in Richmond, Surrey?
Is He at home in these other places? Where is God at home? There
are thousands of living stones, many, many dear believers with
real experience of the Lord, but where has the ark come home?
Where are the staves being lengthened that God has finally come
home? In God Wants a House Lance looks into this desire of the
Lord, this desire He has to dwell with His people. What would
this dwelling look like? Let's seek the Lord, that we can say with
David, "One thing have I asked of Jehovah, that will I seek after:
that I may dwell in the house of Jehovah all the days of my life,
To behold the beauty of Jehovah, And to inquire in his temple."